W9-ACU-758

WORLD ALMANAC® LIBRARY OF THE MIDDLE AGES

knights, Castles, and Warfare

IN THE MIDDLE AGES

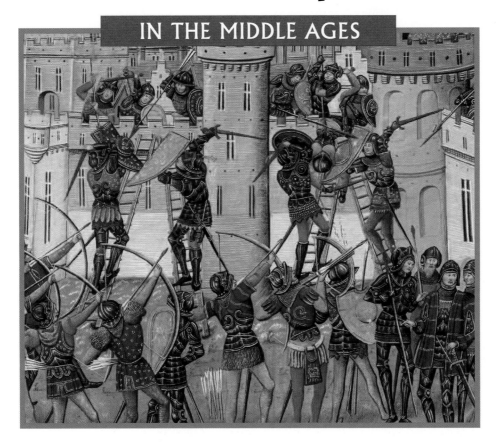

FIONA MACDONALD

WORLD ALMANAC® LIBRARY

Please visit our web site at: **www.garethstevens.com**
For a free color catalog describing World Almanac® Library's list of high-quality books, call 1-800-542-2595 (USA) or 1-800-387-3178 (Canada).

Library of Congress Cataloging-in-Publication Data

Macdonald, Fiona.
    Knights, castles, and warfare in the Middle Ages / by Fiona Macdonald.
        p. c.m. — (World Almanac Library of the Middle Ages)
    Includes bibliographical references and index.
    ISBN-10: 0-8368-5895-6 (lib. bdg.)
    ISBN-13: 978-0-8368-5895-2 (lib. bdg.)
    ISBN-10: 0-8368-5904-9 (softcover)
    ISBN-13: 978-0-8368-5904-1 (softcover)
    1. Knights and knighthood—Juvenile literature. 2. Castles—Juvenile literature.
3. Military art and science—History—Medieval, 500–1500—Juvenile literature.
4. Civilization, Medieval—Juvenile literature. I. Title. II. Series.
    CR4513.M328   2005
    909.07—dc22   2005043267

This North American edition first published in 2006 by
World Almanac® Library
An imprint of Gareth Stevens Publishing
1 Reader's Digest Road
Pleasantville, NY 10570-7000 USA

Produced by White-Thomson Publishing Ltd.
Editor: Walter Kossmann
Designer: Malcolm Walker
Photo researcher: Amy Sparks
World Almanac® Library editorial direction: Valerie J. Weber
World Almanac® Library editor: Jenette Donovan Guntly
World Almanac® Library art direction: Tammy West
World Almanac® Library graphic design: Kami Strunsee
World Almanac® Library production: Jessica Yanke and Robert Kraus

Photo credits:
Akg-Images pp. 8, 9, 12, 20, 24, 25, 28 (British Library, London), 16 (Heiner Heine), cover and 31 (Jerome da Cunha), 11, 18, 27 (Eric Lessing), 21, 26b, title page and 29 (Private Collection), 23 (VISIOARS); Art Archive pp. 32 (Bibliothéque Nationale Paris), 40 (British Library), 26t (Joseph Martin), 7 (Museo Civico Padua/Dagli Orti); Bridgeman Art Library pp. 38 (Bargello, Florence), 15 (John Bethell), 36 (Biblioteca Marciana, Venice, Giraudon), 4, 35, 37, 43 (British Library, London), 13 (British Museum, London), 5 (Chateau de Pierrefonds, France, Peter Willi), 10 (Museo Arqueologico Nacional, Madrid, Lauros/Giraudon), 39 (Private Collection); Topfoto pp. 17 (AAAC/Topfoto), 19.

Cover: English and French knights charge each other at the Battle of Patay in 1429.
Title page: Arrows are shot over a besieged town's walls in France in c. 1450.

Printed in the United States of America

2 3 4 5 6 7 8 9 10 09 08 07

Contents

Words that appear in the glossary are printed in **boldface** type the first time they occur in the text.

Source References on page 45 give bibliographical information on quoted material. See numbers ([1]) at the bottom of quotations for their source numbers.

he Middle Ages are the period between ancient and early modern times—the years from about A.D. 500 to 1500. In that time, Europe changed dramatically. The Middle Ages began with the collapse of the **Roman Empire** and with "**barbarian**" tribes invading from the north and east. In the early years of the Middle Ages, western European farmers struggled to survive. This period ended with European merchants eagerly seeking new international markets, European travelers searching for lands and continents unknown to them to explore, European artists creating revolutionary new styles, and European thinkers developing powerful new ideas in religion, government, and philosophy.

What Were the "Middle Ages" Like?

Some people view the period as the "Dark Ages," an era marked by ignorance and brutality. It is true that **medieval** people faced difficult lives marred by hard work, deadly diseases, and dreadful wars, but their lives included more than that.

The Middle Ages were also a time of growing population, developing technology, increasing trade, and fresh ideas. New villages and towns were built; new fields were cleared; and, with the help of new tools like the wheeled iron plow, farms produced more food. **Caravans** brought silks and spices from faraway lands in Asia. New sports and games, such as soccer, golf, chess, and playing cards, became popular. Musicians, singers,

A HISTORIAN'S VIEW

"A hundred years ago the medieval centuries . . . were widely regarded as 'The Dark Ages.' . . . It was an age whose art was barbaric or 'Gothic'—a millennium of darkness—a thousand years without a bath. Today . . . scholarship [has] demonstrated clearly that the medieval period was an epoch of immense vitality and profound creativity."
C. Warren Hollister [1]

acrobats, and dancers entertained crowds at fairs and festivals. Traveling troupes performed plays that mixed humor with moral messages for anyone who would stop and listen.

Religion, education, and government all changed. Christianity spread throughout Europe

◀ Dressed in full armor and riding a splendid horse, a knight bids farewell to his wife and daughter-in-law before riding off to fight—and perhaps to die. They hand him his helmet and shield and wish him good luck.

◄ Two massively strong stone towers guard the entrance to Pierrefonds Chateau (castle) in France, built between 1392 and 1407. Like other late medieval castles, it served as a fortress, **garrison**, and luxurious home for French nobles.

and became more powerful. Another major faith—Islam—was born and carried into Europe from the Middle East. New schools and universities trained young men as scholars or for careers in the Church, medicine, and the law. Medieval rulers, judges, and ordinary citizens created **parliaments**, jury trials, and the common law. These changes in the fabric of society still shape our world today.

Historians divide the entire period into two parts. In the early Middle Ages, from about A.D. 500 to 1000, Europe adjusted to the changes caused by the fall of the Roman Empire and the formation of new kingdoms by Germanic peoples. In these years, the Christian Church took form and Europeans withstood new invasions. In the late Middle Ages, from about 1000 to 1500, medieval life and culture matured. This period saw population growth and economic expansion, the rise of towns and universities, the building of great cathedrals and mosques, and the launching of the **Crusades**.

Constant Conflict

Through all the exciting changes of medieval times, one aspect of life stayed the same. Someone, somewhere in Europe, was always fighting a war. The fight might have been a local feud between neighboring farmers and their families, a result, for example, of sheep stealing. It might have been a fight between great nobles over who should inherit a castle or between rival princes for the right to be king. Or it might have been a massive crusade against non-Christians, championed by the Christian Church, which inspired thousands of devout soldiers to risk death in a foreign land.

A wide variety of soldiers fought most medieval wars. Medieval soldiers ranged from brutal **Viking** pirates and wild, fierce **Goths** and **Huns** to noble, chivalrous **knights** on horseback, attended by pages and **squires** from noble or wealthy families. Few medieval kingdoms had organized citizen armies. Instead, rulers relied on trained, trusty warriors, noble lords, and rich landowners to recruit ordinary foot soldiers to fight for them. By the end of the Middle Ages, there were also private armies of **mercenary** troops who would fight for anyone who paid them.

Women and children did not usually fight in wars, but they suffered all the same. They were trapped inside castles or walled towns and were left to starve by enemies. They were robbed, raped, and massacred by hostile soldiers marching through their lands. They grieved—and often faced hardship—when their menfolk died.

Medieval knights and foot soldiers fought because they felt they must—to defend their homes and families, drive off enemies, obey royal orders, or win treasure and land. Always, war was bloody and brutal, but medieval people believed it could, just occasionally, be glorious, as well.

CHAPTER 1

What knights did

oems written in the Middle Ages contain many descriptions of the perfect knight. He was a soldier of noble birth. He was brave, wise, courteous—and handsome. Bold and bloodthirsty on the battlefield, he loved poetry and music when at home. A devout Christian, he was also inspired by romantic love. Most important of all, he was a good comrade. His motto was "Loyalty binds me."

Of course, this ideal knight did not exist, but the poems describing him and praising his brave deeds tell us how some medieval people liked to view soldiers, fighting, and war.

CHIVALROUS KNIGHT

"A knight there was, and he a worthy man,
Who, from the moment that he first began
To ride about the world, loved chivalry,
Truth, honor, freedom and all courtesy."
Geoffrey Chaucer, late 1300s [2]

The First Knights

The reality was quite different from the poetry. The first knights, who lived between A.D. 500 and 1000, were rough, tough fighting men. They joined private armies led by local warlords or rival kings. At that time, Europe was divided into many small, warring states. Invaders also threatened the region: Vikings from northern Europe, which are **Scandinavian** lands; and **nomadic** tribes, such as the Huns and **Magyars**, from Central Asia.

In those dangerous days, a knight's task was to protect his leader's lands and people. He had to be a skillful fighter. He had to obey his leader's orders—even if that meant death. He had to be rich enough to own a horse, weapons, and armor. He had to leave his family and spend months living in forts and army camps. He might have had to make long, risky journeys by land or sea. In return for such loyal service, a knight's leader—also known as his lord—gave him generous gifts of land plus rights to control the people who lived there.

Feudalism

According to medieval laws, all land belonged to kings. In practice, the king might not have occupied large parts of his kingdom. He gave land to other people in return for essential services. This practice is sometimes called "feudalism," or the "feudal system," after *feodum*—the Latin word for "grant."

Kings gave large **estates** to important lords who promised to fight alongside them and bring knights and foot soldiers to aid them in any battles. Lords gave smaller estates to their knights in return for fighting when called upon. Knights gave fields to **peasants** in return for a share of farm crops grown on their farms or for

IDEAL LOYALTY

"It is a joyful thing, war. . . . You love your comrades so much in war. A great sweet feeling of loyalty and sympathy fills your heart when you see your comrade so bravely risking his life. . . . And then you are willing to live or die with him, and for brotherly love not to abandon him. . . . Do you think that a man who experiences this fears death? No! He feels so strengthened, so 'high' that he does not know where he is. Truly, he fears nothing."
Fifteenth-century French writer

▶ The ideal knight is pictured in a manuscript from the end of the Middle Ages. He is richly dressed, with golden spurs, and his horse wears a trapper (blanket) decorated with the knight's coat of arms (badge of a noble family).

rent paid in money. Lords promised to protect the king's territory, and their own estate, land, and people. Apart from sheltering in their lord's castle in wartime, however, most peasants received little practical help from their lords.

New Peacetime Duties

The first knights were feared as brutal warriors. They won respect for their strength and daring. Fighting was their whole life's work. Later in the Middle Ages, however, about 1000, knighthood began to change. Many knights still served in their lord's armies and maintained their own private teams of fighting men, but they also spent time at home, managing their estates or taking part in politics. Some were summoned to be members of parliaments; others served as law-keepers in their local communities. Several knights paid a special tax, called "scutage," to be excused from fighting altogether.

At the same time, knights became known by respectful titles such as "sir" (in English) or "chevalier" (in French). Knights' wives shared in their husband's status and were called "dame" or "madame." As befitted their high **rank**, knights were expected to be gracious, honorable, and just. However "civilized" their behavior, though, most knights remained tough warriors at heart.

Medieval Kings

As landowners, knights and their lords belonged to a rich, privileged elite—the top 10 percent of the population. Other members included kings, bishops or senior clergy, and leading merchants. The rest of medieval society— peasant farmers and ordinary townsfolk—were poor and disadvantaged.

Medieval kings claimed to be God's deputies on Earth. They demanded loyalty, reverence, respect, and obedience. It was their duty to defend their

▼ Peasant farmers use sickles (large curved knives) to harvest ripe grain. At left, a reeve (official employed by a land-holding lord) gives orders. The big stick is a sign of his rank and power. This image was made in England, around 1325.

MEMORIES OF A KING WHO RULED WELL, 843

"In the times of Charles the Great of good memory, who died almost 30 years ago, peace and harmony ruled everywhere. . . . But now everyone goes their own separate way, and quarrels and fighting are everywhere."
Nithard [3]

King Philip II of France (*center left*) meets bishops (senior clergy, right, with pointed hats) to discuss politics in 1188. Two royal servants stand behind the king, ready to carry out his commands.

kingdoms, promote peace and prosperity, and make good laws. To pay for royal government, they collected tolls and taxes. Kings relied on lords and knights for support and advice, and to help manage their kingdoms. They often quarreled with strong-minded or too-powerful advisers, however, or were betrayed by ambitious noble families who wanted to gain power.

The Church

In medieval times, the Christian Church was very rich, with great political and spiritual influence. Its wealth came from land, treasure, and magnificent buildings, all given by medieval people to show their devotion to God. Everyone—from kings and knights to peasants—believed that without help from the Church, they could not get into heaven.

Priests and monks were the best-educated people in Europe. They worked as lawyers, clerks, and government officials. Top clergy played an important part in politics. They called on kings, lords, and knights to fight against the Church's enemies—from **Muslim** invaders to quarrelsome

ST. BERNARD OF CLAIRVAUX ENCOURAGES KNIGHTS:

"Go forward . . . knights, and with fearless souls drive away the enemies of the cross of Christ, certain that neither death nor life can separate you from the love of God. . . . How glorious are the winners who return safely from battle! How blessed are the martyrs who die fighting! Life is fruitful, victory is splendid . . . but death [in battle] is better than either of these things."

Christian rulers. The clergy performed special rituals to bless knights going to war. At the same time, the clergy told the knights to set a good example by obeying the Church's moral teachings.

Warring Kingdoms

In early medieval times, all kings were war leaders whose aim was to make their kingdoms bigger and richer by conquering more land. They often had to fight to win or stay in power. In many lands, all of the king's sons had the right to claim the throne. The strongest warrior usually won.

After the Roman Empire collapsed, in about A.D. 476, rival kings fought for a share of Roman lands. In 800, King Charlemagne, who ruled in what is now France, Italy, and Germany, founded what he called a **Holy Roman Empire** and

CALLED UP FOR THE HOLY ROMAN EMPEROR, 1422

"Duke of Lorraine 20 swordsmen [knights]
Duke of Bar 20 swordsmen
Duke of Savoy 50 swordsmen
Margrave of Baden 10 swordsmen
Landgrave of Hesse 20 swordsmen, 10 men-at-arms [foot soldiers]
Duke Otto 10 swordsmen, 10 men-at-arms
Erich of Brunswick 5 swordsmen, 5 men-at-arms
Duke Otto of Hirschberg 5 swordsmen, 5 men-at-arms
Duke of Berg 6 spearmen."

proclaimed himself emperor of all Christian lands. Other German rulers later claimed the title of emperor and ruled some of Charlemagne's lands. The rest of the western Roman Empire was divided among other new kingdoms in Britain, France, Spain, and Italy. The eastern regions of the Roman Empire formed the Byzantine Empire by the end of the fourth century.

At the same time, beginning about A.D. 370, hostile tribes from the north and east caused massive destruction throughout Europe. Some, like the **Visigoths** who attacked Spain, settled and founded new kingdoms. Others, like the Huns and **Vandals**, raided the European countryside and then rode away. Their invasions forced European peoples out of their old homelands. The **Angles** and **Saxons** from Germany, for example, had to settle in Britain.

Later, about A.D. 700, new invaders attacked. Muslims from North Africa took control of southern Spain, founding Muslim states that survived there until 1492. Muslim farmers from North Africa settled in Spain. Then Muslim armies advanced north, through France, until **Frankish** (northern French) knights defeated them at the Battle of Poitiers in 732.

◀ A Visigoth king in Spain gave this jeweled crown to the Christian Church as an offering of thanks. The Visigoths were wild tribes from Germany who attacked Rome in 410 and a few years later attacked and finally settled in Spain.

hero Roland

Roland, a Frankish knight, was the most famous warrior of his day. In real life, he died in 778 fighting **Basque** warriors from Spain. Medieval writers turned the story of his life and death into an exciting epic although they changed many details to fit in with their own religious and political ideas. They claimed Roland was killed in a battle with Muslim invaders and that he had a magic sword that contained relics (remains) of Christian saints.

▼ Norman knights on horseback attack Anglo-Saxon foot soldiers at the Battle of Hastings, 1066. This image comes from the Bayeux Tapestry, a huge embroidered wall hanging, made by Norman women around 1080. Above the knights are ravens, ready to feed on the corpses of dead soldiers, shown at the bottom of the picture.

Vikings and Magyars

From A.D. 800 to 1100, Vikings, warriors from Scandinavia, terrorized Europe. They sailed in fast "dragon ships" to raid coastal villages and **migrated** to new settlements they made from Iceland to Sicily. They fought against Christian kings, such as Alfred the Great (ruled 849–899) of Wessex, England, and founded the first kingdom in Russia. In France, Vikings established the powerful duchy (state ruled by a duke) of Normandy. In 1066, Duke William of Normandy, who had Viking ancestors, invaded and conquered England.

Magyar nomads from the Volga River region (now in Russia) invaded eastern Europe. In A.D. 955, knights led by Holy Roman Emperor Otto the Great (ruled 912–973) halted their advance toward German lands. In 1000, a new Magyar

kingdom (now Hungary) was founded, to the east of Otto's lands. The Magyars were converted to Christianity by Stephen, the kingdom's first king.

After about 1000, the mass migration of peoples from one region to another subsided considerably in Europe. European communities began to settle down within fixed boundaries. They still fought each other, however. For example, from 1337 to 1453, Britain and France clashed in the Hundred Years War, with the kings of both countries claiming the right to rule southwestern France. Late medieval kingdoms were also torn apart by bitter civil wars. The Wars of the Roses in Britain (fought 1455–1485 between the house of York and the house of Lancaster for the English throne) brought death to hundreds of knights and at least four kings. The largest, most dramatic medieval conflicts after 1000, however, involved enemies outside Europe.

Crusaders

The Crusades were religious wars between Christians and non-Christians. They were fought against **pagans** in northern Europe, **heretics** in France, and Muslims in the Middle East. Christian and Muslim rulers both wanted to control the Holy Land (the area where Jesus Christ once lived). This land was sacred to Christians, Muslims, and Jews. Since A.D. 636, Muslims had ruled it, but Jewish and Christian people had lived peacefully alongside them. Then, after

Jihad

Jihad is an Arabic word meaning "effort" or "struggle" to devote oneself to God.
Medieval Muslims used it to describe:
- trying to live a good life
- trying to create a good community
- trying to protect or spread the faith of Islam, by fighting, if necessary.
Medieval Muslims believed Jihad was their duty and it often led to war.

▼ King Philip II of France (ruled 1180–1223) was one of the most famous Christian leaders during the Crusades. This medieval manuscript illustration shows him being offered homage (loyalty) by English soldiers (right), led by Richard the Lion-Heart, as they leave the ships that have brought them to the Holy Land.

about 1000, new, less tolerant Muslims began to rule, and warlike Muslim tribesmen—the Seljuk Turks—threatened to invade nearby Christian lands in eastern Europe.

In 1095, Pope Urban, leader of the Roman Catholic Church, called on Christians to defend the Holy Land. Many lords, knights, and ordinary people hurried to join the Crusades. This took great courage. Volunteers knew they would probably die overseas. They made their wills, said goodbye to their families, and set sail.

The Crusades lasted from 1096 to 1493. At first, the Christians were successful. They captured the holy city of Jerusalem and set up a Christian kingdom there, but Muslim armies led by a brilliant **Kurdish** general called Saladin (his full name was Salah-ad-Din Yusuf ibn Ayyub) reconquered Jerusalem in 1187. Muslims finally drove Christian lords, knights, and foot soldiers out of the Holy Land by 1291. Later Crusaders failed to win back Jerusalem, but they did defeat heretics in southern France and converted pagan peoples in Prussia, Lithuania, and other Baltic states to Christianity, many by force.

World Rulers?

Just a few years earlier, in the 1240s, a new enemy—**Mongol** nomads from Central Asia—threatened Christians and Muslims in eastern Europe. In 1206, Mongol tribes united under a new leader, Genghis Khan, and set out to conquer the world. Mongol warriors, armed with bows and arrows and riding small, swift horses, took control of what is now Russia in 1237. Next, they defeated an army of German and Polish knights in 1241. It seemed as if they would conquer all Europe. Quarrels among their leaders eventually caused them to retreat, however. Even so, Mongols ruled what is now Russia for two hundred years.

▶ This image, from a fifteenth-century Persian (present-day Iranian) manuscript shows Genghis Khan and his Mongol soldiers at war. They are all riding small, swift ponies and are armed with bows and arrows—the Mongols' favorite, deadly weapons.

DESCRIPTION OF THE MONGOLS, 1260

"What army in the whole world can equal the Mongol army? It is an army of ordinary men—but also ordinary men joined together in an army. All of them, great and small, noble and lowborn, become swordsmen, archers, and spearmen in times of battle."
Juvaini [4]

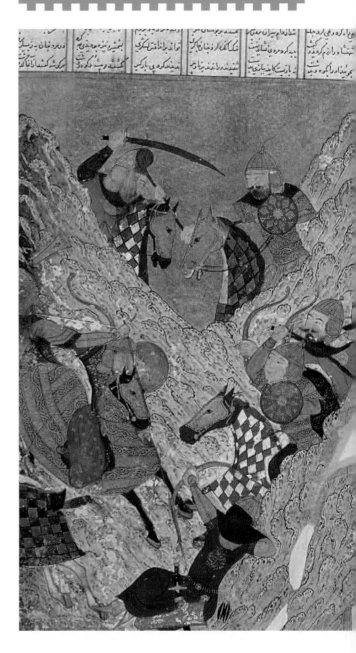

knights and Castles

Throughout the Middle Ages, kings, lords, and knights built castles. They were designed for a time when life was rough, risky, and cruel. They were safe strongholds for surviving a long **siege** or a sudden attack. They were also family homes, proud symbols of power, and bases to shelter armies in enemy land. They advertised a person's rank and riches and protected their dependents, their soldiers, and their estates.

Wooden Buildings

The first castles were built in about A.D. 900. They were made of earth and timber. Some were simply steep, ring-shaped banks of earth, surrounded by deep ditches, with a level open space inside. Others had strong palisades (fences) of upright timber poles on top of the earth bank, to give extra protection.

After about 1050, castle designs changed. Castle builders heaped up earth and stones to create an artificial mound, called a motte. They built a wooden tower on top of the motte surrounded by palisades. Defenders inside this wooden fort stayed out of reach of enemy arrows and safe from charging knights on horseback.

Nearby, on level ground, castle builders cleared a large open space, called a bailey. They guarded this with a wooden fence and, sometimes, an earth bank and a ditch. Inside the bailey, they built wooden huts to store food and water for soldiers in the castle and to shelter horses. Sometimes, they built a wooden hall in the bailey, as well, where off-duty knights and soldiers could spend time. Baileys were linked to mottes by movable wooden bridges or by fenced walkways.

Building in Stone

After about 1100, castles began to be built of stone, with **donjons**, or massive square towers, to replace the earlier wooden forts. Stone was much stronger than wood and did not burn. Stone was scarce, more expensive, and difficult to work with, however. A wooden castle could be

Ready-Made Castles

Invading armies carried ready-made wooden castles with them, in small sections, ready to be put together. These could be assembled to provide safe shelter in enemy territory at very short notice.

built in weeks or even days in an emergency. A typical square stone donjon, with walls 10 feet (3 meters) thick, 50 feet (15 m) high, and 100 feet (30 m) long on each side, took many years to complete.

Castle walls were constructed of stone rubble (roughly shaped chunks) and earth tightly packed together. Ashlar (neatly trimmed stone blocks) was used to cover the inside and outside of each wall. In northern Europe, building was usually only possible for slightly more than half the year, during the warmer, drier months from April to November. Building was possible all year round in southern Europe.

To make donjons even stronger, narrow protective towers were sometimes added at each corner. Later, from about 1150, donjons were round, not square. Round donjons had no corners for enemies to undermine (dig underneath), and so were much less likely to collapse. The sites for stone castles were very carefully chosen. Old-style earth mottes were of no use—they would not bear such a heavy weight. Favorite sites for stone-built castles included rocky crags or mountaintops, as for Chateau Gaillard, in France, for example, or cliffs beside fast-flowing rivers,

▲ Built in the twelfth century, Orford Castle in eastern England, originally had a moat, a curtain wall with flanking towers, and a twin-towered gatehouse. All that remains today is the twenty-one-sided central tower, or keep.

such as the Rhine River in Germany. These sites gave the occupants a commanding view of their surroundings. Foot soldiers found it difficult to climb crags or swim rivers, and knights on horseback found it impossible to reach these castles.

Moats and Walls

Where there were no natural obstacles to keep enemies away, castle builders dug deep artificial

AN ACCOUNTING FOR KING EDWARD I

English castle architect Master James wrote to King Edward I's government officials regarding costs of a building in about 1280:

"In case you ask how we are spending so much money each week, we must tell you that we are using 400 stonemasons [cutters and layers], plus 2,000 skilled laborers. We also need 100 carts, 60 wagons, and 30 boats to bring stone and coal. We employ 20 quarrymen, 30 blacksmiths, and many carpenters. We also have to pay the garrison [soldiers on guard duty]."

moats, as at Bodiam Castle, England, to stop attackers from getting close to the castle walls. Sometimes, the builders added rows of sharp wooden poles in front of the moats, sticking up at an angle from the ground.

After about 1200, thick stone curtain walls up to 30 feet (9 m) high surrounded donjons for security reasons. Often, there was more than one curtain wall. For example, at Caerphilly Castle, Wales, there were two sets, one inside the other. This design is called "concentric." Some

Security Stairs

Castles were tall buildings and had stairways leading from one floor to another. Stairs were built in towers or in spaces hollowed out from stone walls. Like everything else in a castle, stairs were designed for defense. They were mostly built as spirals winding upward in a clockwise direction. This meant that right-handed attackers (the majority) found it difficult to use their swords when climbing a staircase; also, most of their body was easily attacked by defenders above.

historians think Crusader knights brought this design back to Europe from the Middle East. Sometimes, flanking towers were built at intervals around the curtain walls to strengthen them. The towers also served as useful platforms for lookouts and allowed defenders to shoot from several angles at enemies trying to climb in. The walls around Dover Castle, which was used to guard the English Channel, had fourteen flanking towers.

Attackers and defenders all knew that the entrance to a castle was its weakest point. Most castles therefore only had one main door, plus a tiny sally-port (emergency exit) just big enough to crawl through at the opposite side of the building. Castle builders included several different doorway defenses in their designs. Castle doors themselves were made of thick planks of oak—the toughest European wood. They had heavy iron locks and bolts and were strengthened by iron crossbars, or were studded with massive iron nails. These crossbars and nails stopped attackers from smashing their way through. A large castle might have several sets of doors guarding the entrance with sentries stationed in between them on duty twenty-four hours a day. A castle's outer door was often protected by a portcullis, a movable grid of wood

◄ Schloss (castle) Prunn, in Bavaria, Germany, dates from the eleventh century. It was built on a rocky cliff overlooking the wide, fast-flowing Danube River. Its site made it impossible for enemies to make a surprise attack.

▲ The thirteenth-century stone-built gatehouse, deep moat, and movable wooden drawbridge can still be seen today at Hever Castle, in southeast England. All these features helped to defend the castle.

and iron that could be lowered across the entrance and locked into position, barring the door completely.

Castle doors were usually built several feet above ground level. Anyone approaching had to climb a wooden ladder—easily removed in time of danger—or walk across a drawbridge, a sloping walkway that could be hauled up to stop enemies from getting near. All these castle entry

Gatehouses

Gatehouses at castle entrances—either in the outer wall or more often the inner donjon—were often used as jails. No one wanted to let captured enemies too far inside their castle, for fear they might escape and do damage or act as spies and carry back reports of castle defenses to enemies outside.

defenses, guarded by a massive stone gatehouse, had sentry rooms, spy holes, lookout towers, and storage for defenders' weapons.

From Castle to Stately Home

During the fourteenth century, castles began to be built less like forts, and more like palaces or grand, gracious homes. Old castles were remodeled, and new castles were constructed using fresh and different designs. There were two reasons for the change. In spite of battles between rival nations and several civil wars,

▼ The great hall, at Bunratty Castle in Ireland, is typical of many castles built in medieval times. The walls are hung with tapestries, the floor is made of massive stone slabs. A fire burns in a metal brazier (container) in the center of the room. The lord and his guests would have sat on wooden chairs at the only table while others would have been seated on low benches or lounged on the floor.

ADVICE TO DINERS IN A CASTLE GREAT HALL

"Don't scratch yourself.
Don't look for fleas on your chest or in your breeches.
Don't snap your fingers.
Don't comb your hair.
Don't clean your nails.
Don't take off your shoes if noblemen or women are present.
Don't urinate—unless you own the castle. Then you can do anything you like!"
Daniel of Beccles [5]

Europe was a more peaceful place after 1300. Also, new weapons, first used in the fourteenth century, made castle defenses easier to attack and thus no longer useful as fortresses. Castles were no longer so safe or secure.

The early castles were built with just one large living space, called a hall. This occupied the whole main floor of the donjon tower. This main floor was usually on the first floor above the ground floor. A smoky fire burned in the middle of the hall, and dogs usually sniffed and scratched among rushes covering the floor. The castle owner and his family, guests, servants, and soldiers used the hall for eating, talking, relaxing, and sleeping. The owner and his family ate at a special high table, set apart from the crowd, and slept in curtained beds or behind screens. They had no privacy and little peace.

The ground floor of the donjon was used for extra storage. Guards and lookouts patrolled the battlements (fortified tops of the walls). Chapels, kitchens, storerooms, workrooms, and stables were in small wood or stone buildings outside.

Private Lives

Starting in about 1300, space inside old and new castle donjons was divided to create more privacy. Separate rooms called solars, which were usually bedrooms and sitting rooms combined, were made for the knight, his family, and trusted servants, such as the castle chaplain (priest). There were also sitting rooms, called bowers, for women only and private gardens where women and children could enjoy fresh air. New bedchambers were built, with **garderobes**, bathtubs, and fireplaces. Knights often used their chambers as a peaceful place to read or to visit with close friends.

Bedchambers were furnished with four-poster beds, wooden storage chests, religious pictures or statues, and perhaps a bookcase and a comfortable high-back chair. The walls were hung with painted cloth and woven tapestries, which kept out drafts and were decorative. Pictures on wall hangings reminded knights of favorite

▲ Chateau Amboise, in western France, was one of the finest new castles built at the end of the Middle Ages (soon after 1500) as a grand, luxurious home. Amboise was designed as a house for the kings of France to use while they went hunting.

A FIFTEENTH-CENTURY FRENCH KNIGHT'S FAVORITE SPORT

"He spent all his spare time hunting stags. He got up very early, sometimes rode an extremely long way, and would not stop hunting even in terrible weather. When he returned home in the evening he was often totally exhausted, and usually bad-tempered with his companions and the hunt servants, because the hunt did not always go well."
Author's translation

leisure occupations, such as hunting, dancing, and feasting, or portrayed the adventures of brave, famous warriors from long ago.

After about 1300, the great hall of a castle was used just for dining and entertaining guests and for public purposes, such as receiving royal messengers. Soldiers and servants were given separate sleeping quarters, away from the knight and his family. New, better kitchens were built for

▲ A lord and his lady (*second right*) entertain guests at a feast while musicians play lively, cheerful tunes. This image was painted in France in about 1300.

cooking meals and baking bread. Storehouses were enlarged to contain food grown by peasant farmers on the knight's "home farm," purchased from local markets, or carried by cart from distant ports. Old wells were cleaned and fitted with lead pipes to carry water to kitchens and, occasionally, to bedchambers. New workshops for metalworking, woodworking, mending armor, making and fixing saddles and other riding equipment, repairing farm tools, spinning and weaving cloth, and cheesemaking were built and equipped so castle staff could work more efficiently.

Castle Community

Early castles housed kings, lords, knights, and foot soldiers. By about 1300, however, castles had grown so large and elaborate that they needed many servants to run them. The castle staff formed a complete community, with a wide range of skills and duties. Senior staff, like the steward and marshal, were expert administrators in charge of many people and large sums of money. They commanded great respect and often

Servants Working Mostly Indoors

Steward (in charge of castle household)
Chamberlain (in charge of castle finances)
Reeve (in charge of castle farms)
Chaplain (priest)
Tutor
Lawyer
Clerks (secretaries)
Keeper of the wardrobe (in charge of clothes)
Grooms (personal servants)
Ladies' maids and Nursemaids
Cleaners
Head cook (in charge of food) and Baker
Scullions (kitchen servants)
Butler (in charge of drinks)
Taster (checks knight's food for poison)
Ewerer (brings water for washing hands)
Naperer (in charge of silver plates and table linen)
Pages (wait on tables)
Squires
Musicians, Jugglers, and Fools (clowns)

Servants Working Mostly Outside

Marshal (in charge of horses)
Saddler
Farrier and Grooms (care for horses)
Falconer (trains hunting falcons)
Huntsmen
Gardeners
Thatcher (repairs roof thatch)
Carpenter
Stonemason
Handyman
Blacksmith
Storekeepers (manage and store supplies)
Cooper (barrel maker)
Carter (transporter with horse and cart)
Messenger
Spinners and weavers
Laundress
Porter (gatekeeper)
Sweeper
Garderobe-cleaner

◀ A peasant farmer plows a
field with a wooden plow
pulled by oxen in about 1416.
In the distance are more
peasants pruning vines and a
splendid castle, surrounded by
three sets of walls.

came from high-ranking families. Junior staff,
such as sweepers and washerwomen, were
recruited from villages near the castle.

Most servants spent their lives working in
one castle, but senior staff traveled with kings,
lords, and knights when they moved from one
castle to another. The richest medieval families
owned several grand homes. It was a major feat
of organization to move valued belongings safely
and to have the castles ready for the owners
when they arrived. Books, tapestries, silverware,
and fine furniture were all carefully loaded into
large carts pulled by horses or oxen for transport

across the countryside. The castle owner's wife
often played an important part in planning
household moves, working closely with senior
castle staff.

The castle also had links with peasants living
nearby. Some worked on farms belonging to the
knight who owned the castle, growing crops and
raising animals to feed the castle community.
Others paid him rent for their own plots of
land. In war, they sought shelter within the
castle's strong walls. In peacetime, they carried
farm produce to the castle and paid rents and
taxes there.

CHAPTER 3

Ready to fight

t was difficult to become a knight. Only a few people could qualify. The first requirement was to be male. In medieval times, women were not expected to fight, carry weapons, wear armor, or ride horses into battle. In dangerous situations, of course, some women did fight bravely. Traders' wives sometimes joined defenders hurling rocks at enemies from the tops of city walls. Knights' wives often roused staff and servants to defend castles while their husbands were away. Even peasants' wives grabbed **pitchforks** to defend their children and homes from raiders and invaders.

The second requirement for becoming a knight was birth and "breeding." By *breeding,* medieval people meant "upbringing" or "family environment." Usually, only boys from high-ranking families—knights, lords, or royalty—were accepted to be trained as knights. In medieval times, social rank was passed on through inheritance, from father to son. Boys from peasant families or trading families who worked in towns had very little chance of becoming knights.

Training as a Page and a Squire

A boy's training began young—at around eight years old—when he was sent away by his parents to live in a lord's castle. There, along with other boys of around the same age, he was expected to make himself useful as a page (servant). He ran errands, carried messages, and waited on tables. He helped the lord's wife and her maidservants by looking after their lapdogs or helping to carry their trains—the heavy lengths of fabric that trailed on the ground behind rich women's robes. The castle chaplain or family tutor taught him to read and write. He learned social skills, such as welcoming guests and making conversation, by copying the lord's family.

Pages also spent part of each day with castle soldiers, learning how to ride and look after horses, how to handle weapons, and how to fight. They were taught to obey orders quickly and without question, and to be tough, brave, and resourceful.

When a page was about fourteen years old, he began a new stage in his training. He served as squire to the lord or king who was training him. Sometimes, squires began as grooms who cared only for the lord's horses. Originally *squire* meant "shield bearer," but most young squires had many other duties. In peacetime, they made themselves generally useful, accompanying the lord to political meetings and on hunting and **falconry** trips. They learned to dance and, if talented, to play a musical instrument, write

Learning to fight

Boys practiced their battle skills by fighting each other with mock weapons made of wood, which were heavier than metal weapons, but less likely to cause serious injury. Handling the heavy wood helped boys develop strong muscles, especially in the chest and arms. (Medieval knights often had spindly legs because they rode horses rather than walking or running.) If a page could not find a partner, he practiced fighting against a *pell,* a thick wooden pole standing upright in the ground.

▶ Two pages (*bottom right*) carry covered dishes of food to King Charles V of France (*second from right at table*) and his guests in Paris, France, in 1378. Before them are **heralds** with trumpets, announcing the arrival of more guests. The castle steward, who is in charge of the feast, stands in the center.

◀ Fourteenth-century French knights clasp their hands above their heads to keep them out of the way as squires fasten long, sharp swords onto heavy leather belts worn around their waists.

Spurs

According to medieval rules of war, only knights were allowed to wear spurs (metal spikes fixed to a rider's heels, which dug into a horse's sides to make it gallop faster). Medieval people said that a young man who fought bravely had "won his spurs"— that is, he had shown himself worthy to be made a knight.

poetry, or sing. They continued to train for battle, riding bigger horses and learning to use real metal weapons.

In wartime, a squire had important work to do. He rode with his lord's army, helping to organize horses, tents, and weapons. Before a battle, he helped his lord put on armor, checked his weapons, and equipped his warhorse. If the lord was injured in the fighting, the squire brought him back from the battlefield, and gave him first aid.

Swearing Loyalty

Boys spent about seven years as a squire. They gained valuable experience by observing battles and hearing knights talk about strategy and tactics. By the time they reached twenty-one years old, most were ready to become knights.

At first, kings usually awarded knighthoods after a battle, as a reward for exceptional bravery. By the fifteenth century, however, knighthood was also awarded as a sign of royal favor, for example, to members of Parliament. Usually

becoming a knight was marked by special ceremonies. These began in the evening, when the squire took a ritual bath to wash away past sins and mark the start of a new stage in his life. After his bath, the squire put on fresh, clean clothes. Then he went to the castle chapel, where he placed his sword on the altar (holy table) and spent all night awake, in prayer. He prayed for his family, the people who had trained him, and for protection in battle. He also prayed that he would be a brave, loyal knight.

In the morning, he went to the great hall of the castle. The lord who had trained him or the king was waiting there. The squire knelt down before him and promised to serve him faithfully. The lord then tapped him on both shoulders with his sword, saying, "Arise, sir knight!" The new knight fastened on his sword and spurs. Afterward, there was a celebration or feast.

It cost a lot of money to live and equip oneself as a knight. Each knight had to pay for his own

▲ Noble Henry of Monmouth (later King Henry V of England) is knighted on the battlefield by King Richard II of England (in red, on horseback), after fighting bravely against Irish warriors in 1399.

weapons, armor, and warhorses, as well as his own group of fighting men. Some young men could not afford this outlay of money and remained squires for life.

Deadly Weapons

A knight needed to equip himself with five or six deadly weapons—a long sword, a short sword, a mace (ridged lumps of metal, fastened to a wooden pole) or flail (iron balls linked to a wooden or metal handle by a heavy metal chain), a battle-ax (a wedge-shaped metal blade fixed to a long wooden handle), a lance (long spear), and maybe a dagger. Each weapon had a different purpose, but all were designed to kill.

Heraldry

Squires often worked as heralds—carrying declarations of war to enemies or messages between commanders on battlefields. They also learned to recognize different coats of arms, which are badges and patterns worn by lords and knights on their armor, helmets, and shields and by ordinary soldiers on their livery (uniforms handed out to followers by powerful families). These coats of arms became hereditary during the Middle Ages and helped heralds report soldiers who behaved badly. The coats of arms also helped identify dead bodies on the battlefield.

A long sword was a knight's most valuable weapon. It was a sign of knightly rank. The best swords were extremely expensive. Until about 1300, knights chose long, flexible swords, with

▶ These swords were worn by knights or lords fighting in Spain in the thirteenth to fifteenth centuries. The second from the left has its sheath next to it on the right. The second sword from the right with its sheath to the right belonged to the last sultan of Granada.

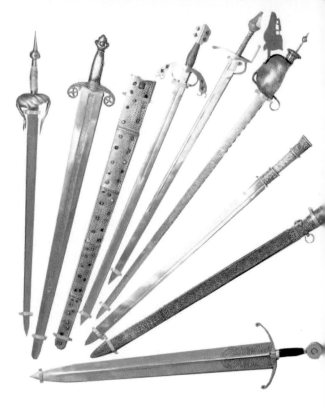

razor-sharp, double-edged blades. They used these for slashing at enemies, cutting right through flesh and bone. The best sword had a big handle so the knight could get a firm grip. Some long swords were so large and heavy that they needed two hands to use them.

Later in the Middle Ages, smaller swords were more popular. They had stiffer, shorter blades, but extra-sharp pointed tips. Knights used them for stabbing through gaps in new-style plate armor (see below and next page). Daggers were also used for stabbing in hand-to-hand fighting on foot. Their slim blades slipped through the smallest chinks in armor.

Knights used both maces and flails to smash enemies over the head. They could cause terrible injuries, even to soldiers wearing helmets. War hammers used by knights fighting on foot were smaller but equally as deadly.

Lances and battle-axes were designed for use by knights on horseback. They could stab or slash right through foot soldiers or throw enemy knights off their horses.

Body Armor

Knights knew that war was very dangerous. They asked God and the saints to watch over them and often carried magic **amulets** or lucky charms. For physical protection, knights wore armor, which was often hot, heavy, and uncomfortable—it trapped perspiration and chafed, but it saved knights' lives.

Styles of armor changed during the Middle Ages, from long chain-mail shirts (worn until about 1350) to plate armor (most popular in the fifteenth century). Chain mail was made of hundreds of tiny metal rings interlinked then riveted together (joined by metal pins). Sometimes, a padded cloth tunic was worn

◀ A chain mail maker named Heintz from Nuremberg, Germany, produces armor for a knight in the fourteenth century. Chain mail is made from interlinking strips of metal and is quite flexible, allowing for movement by the wearer.

▶ This plate armor was made for princes in Germany—and one of their horses—during the fifteenth century. German metalworkers were famous for their skills. Besides creating fine armor, they also made some of Europe's best swords and earliest guns.

underneath. Knights added a helmet and, from about 1200, metal arm and leg protectors.

Plate armor was made of carefully shaped sheets of metal joined together by rivets, leather laces, and sections of chain mail. Worn with a helmet, it covered a knight from head to toe. The best plate armor was tailor-made to fit each individual knight and beautifully decorated with patterns or gilding (covered with a thin layer of gold).

It took at least fifteen minutes—often longer—for a knight, helped by squires, to put on his armor. Chain mail was lighter than plate armor. A typical mail coat weighed about 25 pounds (11.3 kilograms); a suit of armor weighed at least 40 pounds (18.1 kg). Chain mail, however, was

CONTRACT FOR RENTING ARMOR, 1248

"I, Bonfils Manganelli . . . have taken and received from you a certain suit of armor at a rent of seventeen solidi [shillings] which . . . I have already paid you . . . I shall take this armor on the next voyage I am to make across the sea . . . I promise to pay you . . . one augustal [coin] of gold . . . if by chance the armor should be lost through my fault." (The rental fee was about 25 percent of the suit's value.)

more awkward to wear. It hung from the knight's shoulders and dragged him down. The weight of plate armor was more evenly distributed across his body and so felt lighter and easier to move in.

Like weapons, armor was very expensive. Only men from rich families could afford it. Some knights preferred to rent their armor. Armor also was often looted from dead bodies found on the battlefield.

Warhorses

A good warhorse was essential for any knight. Without one, he could not fight properly. Some kings, lords, and the wealthiest knights rode magnificent warhorses called destriers, which were sturdy stallions especially bred to be obedient and aggressive. They often kicked and bit. They were strong enough to carry a knight, his armor, and weapons into battle and brave enough not to run away. Knights who spent a lot

horsemen

In many European languages, the word for knight was, and still is, based on the word for horse. In French, for example, *cheval* means "horse," and *chevalier* (knight) originally meant "horseman." The Italian word for "horse" is *cavallo* and for "knight" is *cavaliere*. English has a similar word, *cavalry*, meaning "soldiers who fight on horseback."

of time fighting needed at least two horses, in case one got injured. They not only had to buy saddles, harnesses, and sometimes horse-armor, they also had to pay to have horseshoes put on.

Knights also needed other kinds of horses for war. Coursers were strong, swift hunters ridden by knights who could not afford destriers. Packhorses and mules (the offspring of a horse mated with a donkey) carried heavy loads of weapons, tents, and food across rough territory.

Carthorses pulled wagons stacked with all kinds of supplies along bumpy medieval roads and carried soldiers who had been injured in battle and were too weak to walk or ride. Palfreys were horses with a steady gait that were comfortable to sit on. Knights chose them for long journeys.

Armed Followers

Knights were elite troops and war leaders. Well trained and disciplined, they were proud of their swordsmanship and horse-riding skills. Most knights fought from a sense of duty—either religious or patriotic. They had chosen fighting as their way of life.

Most of the other men in medieval armies were reluctant recruits. They were peasant farmers or tough laborers who lived in towns. They were asked, or forced, to come to war by kings, lords, and knights. Many were angry at having to leave

◀ William the Conqueror, king of England (1066–1087), is portrayed with his army in an English manuscript of the fourteenth century.

their workshops or farms, but they feared harsh punishments—death if they disobeyed a king's commands or being turned off a lord's or knight's lands. A few volunteered to fight because they had no other means of survival.

Most nobles and knights had to recruit soldiers to fight alongside them in war. Recruiting was part of their feudal duty in return for receiving land from kings. They also had to control, organize, feed, clothe, and reward their fighting men. Medieval soldiers did not get regular wages. Sometimes, they were paid in money; at other times, they were given food or a share of goods looted from enemies.

Almost all ordinary men fought as foot soldiers. They were armed with crude but lethal weapons: wooden sticks and clubs, pitchforks, pikes (pointed blades on long poles), and bows and arrows. Some had valuable fighting skills. In Flanders (now Belgium) and lowland Scotland,

▲ Men with **longbows** shoot arrows over the walls of a besieged town in France in about 1450. The image also shows attacking soldiers climbing ladders and defenders at the top of the town walls ready to grapple with them.

foot soldiers were famous for fighting with pikes. In England, fourteenth-century kings ordered that all peasant men should possess a longbow and should practice shooting with it.

Self-Sacrifice and Self-Defense

Some ordinary people fought for religious reasons. During the Crusades, poor men—and women—joined Christian armies because wandering preachers told them to fight and die for their faith. Other ordinary people fought to protect their homes and families. After about 1300, rich cities recruited militia (citizen soldiers) for defense in wartime. In the country, people stockpiled whatever weapons they could afford and prepared to fight off attackers.

29

CHAPTER 4

In Battle

 eaders of medieval armies did not like fighting battles. They were too dangerous for kings, knights, horses, and ordinary foot soldiers. The fate of an entire army might be decided by one short spell of fighting lasting less than an hour. Attackers often preferred to advance slowly through enemy territory, capturing cities and castles without engaging in actual battles.

Fighting on Horseback

Even so, there were still many battles in medieval times. Knights played an important part in them all. They were the "**shock troops**" of medieval armies. Dressed in armor and mounted on their warhorses, they rode side by side, charging furiously toward enemy knights. Their opponents either stood still in close ranks or began to charge toward them.

As they charged, knights held their long, heavy lances braced firmly against their sides. They aimed to spear their enemies or knock them off their horses to be trampled to death on the ground. A battle between knights was an awesome sight—brave, bloody, and terrible. The ground shuddered with the thud of hooves. The air was full of the shrieks of frightened horses and the cries of wounded and dying men.

Where possible, army commanders chose battle sites that would give knights an extra advantage. The best was a gentle downward slope; it helped knights reach maximum speed. In a charge, knights kept control of their horses by using painful curb bits (pieces of curved metal fitted inside an animal's mouth). These bits stopped horses from pushing their heads too far forward and galloping away. Knights sat in special high-backed saddles that stopped them from falling over backward as they thrust their lances toward the enemy. By resting their feet in metal stirrups, they could stand up while riding and swing their swords with extra force.

Medieval soldiers tried many tactics to wreck a charge by knights on horseback. On dark nights before a battle, they buried sharp wooden spikes in the ground or dug pits where they expected knights would charge. They scattered caltrops (cruel iron spikes) all over the battlefield to maim horses and men. The spikes pierced deep into flesh and caused dangerous infections. They also set traps for knights by stationing people as targets for attack on the far side of bogs or streams. When the knights charged, their horses floundered or tripped, throwing their riders to the ground or into the water.

RICHARD I AT THE BATTLE OF ARSUR, 1191:

*"The King, seeing his men [knights] break away
From line, and charge into the fray,*

*At once drove spurs into his steed
And forced him to his swiftest speed;*

*Charging without delay, he made
All haste to lend these first troops aid.*

*Swifter than **crossbow** bolt doth fly
He rode, with his bold company*

*Toward the right, where with fierce hand
He fell upon the pagan [Muslim] band*

*With such impetuous [fast and furious] attack
That they were [a]mazed and taken back*

*And from their saddles hurled and thrown
So that like sheaves of grain thick strewn*

Ye had seen them lying on the earth."
Ambroise, a Norman jongleur [6]

In early medieval times, ordinary soldiers who fought on foot were no match for well-armed, mounted knights. When knights charged toward them or hit them from high on horseback with

▲ English and French knights charge toward each other on warhorses at the Battle of Patay, France, in 1429. Specially chosen knights on each side carry banners with each nation's royal coat of arms. The French banners have gold fleurs-de-lis only on a blue background.

the Battle of Crécy, france, 1346

The Battle of Crécy was one of the most important battles of the Hundred Years War, a long series of wars between France and England, fought from the 1330s to the 1450s. It was won by English foot soldiers, armed with longbows, who slaughtered French knights on horseback as they charged toward them. More than 1,500 French horsemen were killed, including all the leading French nobles. Many crossbowmen from Genoa, Italy, who were fighting for France, were also killed. Only forty English soldiers died. After Crécy, French armies began to copy the English and fought mostly on foot.

sharp swords and battle-axes, they could not run fast enough to get out of the way. Even if the blade missed, foot soldiers could still be trampled to death or seriously injured.

The Infantry Revolution

Soon after 1300, groups of well-trained foot soldiers showed that they could defeat knights on horseback, after all, by using simple weapons in a new way. These foot soldiers (sometimes called "infantry") were recruited from ordinary people. Unlike knights, they did not need expensive horses. Their weapons were also cheap—some were even homemade—but they changed medieval warfare forever.

In 1302, at the Battle of Courtrai, foot soldiers from the rich trading towns of Flanders (now Belgium) stood shoulder to shoulder in rows, holding long wooden poles tipped with lethal metal spikes. They gave these weapons a cruel nickname: *goedendags* ("good days"). When

◀ At the Battle of Crécy in 1346, French knights (*left*) turn and gallop away to escape arrows shot by English longbowmen. An Italian soldier shoots with a slow, heavy crossbow (*front center*). If a knight fell from his horse in battle, he had to fight hand to hand like any ordinary soldier. His armor, which was hot and heavy, slowed him down considerably.

French knights charged toward them, the men from Flanders stood firm, and the knights and their horses met a horrible death. Any knight who survived the charge became a target for more foot soldiers waiting behind the front ranks, ready to strike out with daggers, heavy clubs, or swords. In 1314, Scottish soldiers defeated English knights in the same way at the Battle of Bannockburn, Scotland. Armed with pikes (sharp blades on long poles) they grouped themselves into bristling schiltrons (circles of pike men facing outward).

It took great courage for foot soldiers to stand firm when faced with charging knights on horseback, but this was the safest option. French writer Jean de Bueil advised his comrades, soon after 1400: "A formation on foot should never march forward, but should always hold steady and await its enemies. . . . Troops which retreat before another force will be defeated, unless God grants them grace."

At first, charging knights could not believe that massed ranks of foot soldiers would not run away. And, once they had started to charge, it was almost impossible for them to stop or change direction. They risked colliding with nearby riders or being thrown off their horses to die as their comrades charged on.

Also in about 1300, English army commanders pioneered new ways of using massed ranks of foot soldiers armed with traditional longbows to shoot a "killer rain" of arrows at charging knights. Longbows were made of tough, springy yew wood and strung with cords of twisted hemp or flax. The largest bows were as tall as a man and could shoot arrows to wound soldiers and horses over 1,000 feet (305 m) away. At closer range, they could kill. A trained archer could shoot at least five arrows in the time it took a knight on horseback to gallop out of range.

Siege Warfare

Open-field battles between knights and foot soldiers could win—or lose—a war, but they were no use for capturing castles or walled cities. If invaders could not get control of castles or cities, they stood little chance of conquering the surrounding land. To capture them, they planned sieges.

During a siege, hostile troops surrounded a castle or city. They stopped anyone from entering or leaving and blocked roads, paths, and rivers to stop enemy armies from attacking the besiegers from behind. Then they waited for months or years until supplies of food and water inside the city or castle were used up. At the same time, they did all they could to kill and injure the inhabitants and force their way through the gates or smash down the walls.

Besieging armies dug tunnels under stonework, propped them up with wood, then lit fires inside. When the wood burned, the tunnel collapsed and the stonework above crumbled and cracked. They hurled rotting meat over the walls to spread disease. They sent spies and assassins to climb in secretly. They poisoned wells and streams. They

frightened besieged people by throwing bodies of dead defenders over the walls as a warning of their own fate. The families of dead soldiers were deeply distressed to see their loved ones used in this way.

Attackers built massive machines called siege engines that threatened the strongest defenses. Battering rams, or huge tree trunks tipped with iron, were one type of siege machine. They swung backward and forward to smash holes in doors and walls. Another type, mangonels, were giant catapults that shot lumps of rock through the air. Trebuchets threw stone missiles, using a seesaw action instead of a catapult. As one end was pulled down, the other swung up, releasing its deadly cargo. Belfries were giant wooden towers. They provided a sheltered platform from which enemy bowmen could shoot at people in castles and cities.

Being besieged was a terrible experience. The trapped people were cold, hungry, dirty, and very frightened. They were cut off from their friends and allies and from news of the outside world. Every day, they faced a terrible choice. Should they stay inside and fight their attackers by shooting arrows or by pouring boiling water over them? Or should they surrender? If they stayed inside, they might starve to death or die from disease, but if they surrendered, or if besiegers broke in, they would probably all be massacred.

The besieged castle's or city's stocks of food and fuel usually ran very low, and they were cut off from fresh drinking water from nearby rivers and streams. Packed tightly together, with little fresh air and almost no chance to exercise, they fell ill with infectious diseases—from the common cold to life-threatening diarrhea. Fear made them feel worse and weakened them to illness of all kinds.

THE SIEGE OF LIMOGES, FRANCE, 1370

The Siege of Limoges was an important event during the Hundred Years War. Attacking English armies had to capture cities like Limoges if they were to win control of the surrounding countryside.

"[Edward] the Black Prince's miners [people who dug under the walls] said, 'Sir, whenever it shall please you we can make part of the city wall fall into the moat, then you can enter into the city at your ease without any danger.' These words greatly pleased the prince. . . . Then the miners lit fires in their mine, and the next morning . . . a great slab of wall fell down. Then the prince . . . and all the other knights with their armies entered into the city . . . ready to do evil. . . . It was pitiful to see the men, women, and children that kneeled down to ask . . . for mercy; but he was so inflamed with anger, that he took no notice of them . . . all were put to death, though they were all innocent. . . . More than three thousand were stabbed or beheaded that day. God have mercy on their souls."
Jean Froissart, a fourteenth-century Flemish writer [7]

▶ In this image, a castle is under siege in about 1350. The attackers are armed with crossbows and a trebuchet (*front left*). They are also using ladders to try to climb over the castle walls. In the background are the tents that belong to the besieging army's commanders.

On Campaign

One of the greatest difficulties facing medieval army commanders was moving troops to battle zones. They had to find food and water for soldiers, provide them with shelter, and keep them safe from enemy attack. Sometimes, commanders had to provide ships to carry a whole army overseas. They also needed to transport weapons, armor, tents, flags, and medical supplies. If the army had won victories, there might also be chests full of treasure.

Medieval armies moved very slowly because most soldiers traveled on foot. Led by knights on horseback, they marched in a ragged line, carrying spare clothes and weapons. Other foot soldiers walked alongside lumbering carts or guided baggage trains of horses and mules.

Each knight was responsible for leading and feeding his own troop of fighting men. He also tried to maintain discipline, making sure that unwilling recruits did not run away, or that soldiers did not get drunk, attack civilians, or loot property. According to medieval priests, who drew up rules for fair wars, soldiers were only meant to fight other armed men.

Almost always, the rules of fair wars were broken. Hungry soldiers raided villages and farms, stealing food from local farmhouses, kidnapping farm animals to cook and eat, or pulling up vegetables growing in the fields.

▼ Soldiers (*left*) ride through enemy territory in about 1350. The soldiers move slowly, following a lumbering cart laden with barrels of food and drink and pulled by a team of sturdy mules.

They also stole anything valuable they could find to take home with them or barter for food and drink when they came to the next friendly town. All too often, they attacked women and children, set fire to houses and barns, and killed any men who tried to defend their homes and families. Sometimes, army commanders encouraged these outrages as part of a terror campaign. They hoped to scare enemy kings and knights into surrendering. For example, during the Hundred Years War, the English took part in *chevauchées* (horseback raids) through the French countryside, burning, looting, raping, and killing.

▲ A medieval woman (*bottom right*) bravely confronts an enemy soldier, about 1390. He is threatening to burn down her house by setting fire to it with the burning brand (wooden stick) that he holds in his hand.

A POEM WRITTEN IN NORTHERN FRANCE, c. 1150

"A shudder of fear sweeps through the land. Wherever you look, there are shining helmets and waving flags; the whole country seems covered with men on horseback."
Author's translation

CHAPTER 5

Arts of War

edieval wars were brutal and thousands of knights died in them, but that did not stop the rest from fighting. For some knights, war was also a passion, an entertainment, and a sport. They took part in jousts and **tournaments**—mock fights and battles. These were often staged with elaborate ceremony.

Training for War

The first tournaments were held soon after 1000. Their purpose was to help knights practice battle skills. Two teams of eleven men, armed with lances, charged at each other on horseback. Fighting was rough and losing teams had to pay very costly penalties, such as giving up their armor. Both sides took prisoners who were only set free after a **ransom** had been paid—just as in wartime. These first tournaments were dangerous. So many knights were killed or injured that the Church tried to ban the tournaments altogether.

After about 1200, tournaments became gentler. Knights still tried their best to defeat the enemy team, but they fought with blunted weapons to win prizes. The area where battles took place, called "the lists," was much smaller than before, and seats were built around it for important spectators, including kings, lords, and some noblewomen. They were thrilled by the speed and strength of horses and fighting men and excited by the risk of danger. Kings passed laws to stop tournaments from turning into real fights and to make sure contestants fought fairly.

Single Combat

At about the same time, a new kind of mock battle became popular. Jousting was fought between two knights only instead of a group. Each tried to knock the other off his horse. At first, they fought with battle-sharp lances, but these proved so dangerous that blunted ones were used instead. Even so, horses often collided (historians have estimated that they crashed into

▲ This beautiful knight's helmet was made in southern Germany at the end of the medieval period.

each other at a combined speed of over 60 miles (97 km) per hour), and knights were still killed. Soon after 1400, a wooden barrier, called a tilt, was built down the middle of jousting lists to keep charging knights apart.

Some knights entered jousts because they loved fighting; others wanted to prove themselves fit for battle or make a brave display in front of fashionable ladies. They wore love tokens, such as ladies' gloves, on their helmets. A few knights became professional fighters, traveling around the countryside and challenging other men to fights in hope of defeating them and winning a fortune.

Some made their fortunes; others met their deaths. For example, Geoffrey of Brittany, the younger brother of King John of England, fell to the ground and was trampled to death by horses' hooves as he took part in a tournament in Paris, France, in 1186. Another famous fighter, William le Marshal, was once found after a tournament with his head on a blacksmith's anvil. The smith had to beat William's helmet back into shape with a hammer before it could be removed.

A FIFTEENTH-CENTURY JOUST

*"The two knights . . . marched into the arena wearing so much armor that they needed
no further protection. They were handed their swords, lances and battle-axes. Then each
knight climbed on an excellent horse, and positioned himself at about a bow-shot's
distance from his opponent. From time to time, they made their horses prance gallantly,
because they knew everyone was looking at them. . . . They peered at each other closely
through the visors [face-guards] of their helmets, then spurred their horses into action . . .
they struck each other such mighty blows that Sir Reginald's lance was shattered into
four sections which flew up into the air, higher than anyone could have thrown them."*
Author's translation

DESCRIPTION OF A CRUSADER LEADER c. 1150

"He . . . was a religious man, mild-mannered, moral, and God-fearing. He was just, he avoided evil, he was trustworthy and dependable. . . . He was devoted to prayer and holy good deeds, famous for his generosity, gracious, friendly, civil, and merciful. He was tall . . . with big strong limbs, a manly chest, and a handsome face. . . . Everyone thought he was the best at fighting with weapons."

Chivalry

Jousts and tournaments both glamorized war as did a powerful medieval idea called chivalry. Chivalry was a code of good behavior that the ideal knight was supposed to follow. It linked courage and strength with religion and courtly (pure and gracious) love. It was spread by Christian preachers—the Church wanted to make society less violent—and by troubadours (minstrels) from French lords' castles. They made chivalrous knights the heroes of their poems, stories, and songs.

According to priests and minstrels, a chivalrous knight should be religious, wise, brave, and fearless. He should defend the Church, give to the poor, protect the weak, honor women, and be loyal, patient, and persevering. In return, he might hope to win the love of a fair lady, riches on Earth, and a place in heaven. Medieval paintings, manuscripts, tapestries, and many other works of art all contained images of this chivalrous knight.

Death Toll

In real life, war was more likely to bring death than love. New ways of fighting after about 1300 led to many more casualties. Often, just a few knights charging settled earlier battles. They killed, maimed, or scattered the soldiers who faced up to them, but only small numbers of men

◀ ·In about 1450, a young French knight, Jean de Saintré, kneels before a noble lady (*seated left*) to show respect and admiration, while her ladies-in-waiting look on.

were involved on either side. After about 1300, armies of foot soldiers might contain more than ten thousand men. All were at risk of death or injury from pikes, arrows, battle-axes, war clubs, and swords. One of the bloodiest battles ever fought in Britain took place in 1461 at Towton during the Wars of the Roses. About eighty thousand men took part, and almost thirty thousand were killed.

Before they left their castles to go to war, knights made careful preparations. They wrote wills, gave money to charity, and offered gifts to the Church. They gave orders to create lifelike memorial statues so that people would remember them for hundreds of years. (The statues usually showed them in armor with their hands folded in prayer.) Knights also left money to pay for funeral services, with prayers to help their souls reach heaven. The day before a battle, they confessed their sins to a priest and asked God's forgiveness. Confessions meant that their souls were purer—or less wicked—and gave them courage because they believed God would be on their side. Often, mass was said before a battle; just prior to fighting, they usually sang a hymn and said a prayer.

One popular song to sing was a psalm (an ancient song of praise from the Old Testament of the Bible): "Blessed is the Lord my God, who will guide my hand in battle." It was against the Church law for priests to join in fighting, but many clergy, like Guerin, the bishop of Senlis, France, enthusiastically took part in battles. He fought with a mace that killed by bruising and crushing, because the Church taught that it was wrong for priests to kill by shedding blood.

FIFTEENTH-CENTURY POEM; DEATH IS SPEAKING:

*"My dreadful spear is very sharp
Know now that it is ready to strike
No armor can protect you from its wound."*
Author's translation [8]

CHAPTER 6

New Weapons, New Warriors

By the end of the Middle Ages, knights had become less useful. New weapons and new ways of fighting meant that their skills as warriors on horseback were no longer so important. Their armor no longer protected them, and their castles were no longer safe strongholds. After about 1500, soldiers took shelter in new forts designed to withstand the latest weapons. These forts belonged to governments, not individual lords or knights, and were not family homes.

Crossbows and Cannon

After 1300, archers began to use new shooting machines called crossbows. These consisted of a short bow fixed to a heavy wooden stock or support. The bowstring was wound back with a windlass (winding machine) instead of being pulled by hand. This made crossbows extremely powerful. They could fire a metal bolt strong enough to pierce armor and could kill with a single shot. Compared to longbows, crossbows were slow to load and fire, but their power made them very effective, especially against knights and in siege warfare.

Late medieval soldiers also began to use a new invention—the gun. Gunpowder (a mix of chemicals that explodes) was first made in China. It was unknown in Europe until about 1300. After that, however, troops began to carry small harquebuses (handheld guns usually fixed on a support) and to experiment with building massive cannon. Both weapons used gunpowder to shoot metal or stone balls at enemies. Small shot, as balls fired by hand-held guns were called, sunk deep into flesh, causing fatal injuries. Large cannon balls had the power to smash through gates and walls. No castle or city was safe from them.

Pay, Not Loyalty

New ways of recruiting soldiers also made knights less useful. After about 1300, experienced army commanders led private armies of mercenary soldiers. These men fought for anyone who would pay them, without questioning which side in a conflict might be right. They traveled all over Europe to work for many different employers. Some mercenary captains began their careers as knights or inherited a knight's title from their family, but they did not fight as a duty. Unlike earlier knights, they felt no loyalty to their local lord or to their king and country.

Knights still served as army commanders and performed many peacetime duties. They were members of parliament, local judges, royal advisers, and government officials. By about 1500, however, the old feudal way of recruiting and running armies was at an end. The glamour of being a knight, riding to battle on horseback, clad in armor, had become history.

The White Company

Sir John Hawkwood, an English knight, led the White Company, a professional army. He recruited skilled soldiers from the Hundred Years War and led them to fight for rival princes in Italy. His men were well trained, disciplined, and well respected. Many rulers were eager to have them fighting on their side. Hawkwood was so successful that he became the captain general of the army of Florence, one of the most important cities in Italy.

Knighthood Today

Knighthood is still bestowed on male or female citizens of the United Kingdom, the British Commonwealth, or other nations as recognition for exceptional achievement. Politicians, medical professionals, businesspeople, academics, explorers, sports heroes, entertainers, senior civil servants, and charity and humanitarian campaigners have all been made knights. Top military commanders are also awarded knighthood but may get different

▲ Soldiers firing harquebuses besiege a castle in about 1450. Their commander has also brought a fearsome cannon to the siege. It stands on the edge of the castle moat, firing cannonballs made of stone at the castle walls.

awards, such as medals or higher ranks, instead. In theory, knighthood is a gift of the British king or queen, but in fact, it is decided on by a committee of civil servants who are given peoples' names, usually by politicians.

476
The last Roman emperor is forced to flee from Rome, and the western Roman Empire collapses.

732
At the Battle of Poitiers in France, the Franks defeat Muslims invading from Spain.

800
Charlemagne, king of the Franks, takes the title of Holy Roman Emperor.

C. 800-C. 1100
Viking raids take place in many parts of Europe.

C. 900
The first wooden castles are built.

C. 900-1000
Magyars settle in Hungary.

1066
At the Battle of Hastings, the Normans conquer England.

1096-1291
Crusaders try to remove Muslims from the Holy Lands.

C. 1100
The first stone castles are built.

C. 1150
Donjons are built as round, not square, towers.

1187
At the Battle of Arsuf (Arsur), the Muslim leader Saladin captures Jerusalem.

C. 1200
The first "concentric" castles are built with thick stone curtain walls surrounding donjons.

C. 1200-1400
Many new universities are founded.

1206
Mongol tribes unite, led by Genghis Khan.

1209-1229
The crusade against Christian heretics in France takes place.

1237
Mongols take control of what is now Russia.

1241
Mongols invade eastern Europe.

1260
Muslims defeat Mongol invaders in the Middle East.

1277-1283
Edward I of England conquers Wales.

1283-1323
One of the last great fortress castles is built at Caernarfon, Wales.

1302
At the Battle of Courtrai, Flemish foot soldiers armed with pikes defeat French knights on horseback.

1314
At the Battle of Bannockburn, Scots pike men defeat English knights.

1337-1453

The Hundred Years War is fought between England and France.

1346

At the Battle of Crécy, English foot soldiers with longbows defeat French knights.

1347-1351

First, and worst, outbreak of plague spreads throughout Europe; it is known later as the "Black Death."

c. 1350

Cannon are first used in European wars.

1370

Limoges in France is besieged by English soldiers.

c. 1400

Most castles are now built as high-status homes, rather than fortresses.

1429

The French are victorious at the Battle of Patay.

1453

Constantinople, the capital of the Byzantine Empire, is captured by Muslim Turks.

1455

The first Bible is printed by Johannes Gutenberg in Mainz, Germany.

1455-1485

The battles in the Wars of the Roses are fought in England.

1461

The Battle of Towton results in 30,000 deaths.

Source References:

[1] **C. Warren Hollister,** *Medieval Europe: A Short History*, **Wiley, 1964, p. 1.**

[2] **Geoffrey Chaucer,** *Canterbury Tales: The Prologue.*

[3] **Nithard,** *Histories of the Sons of Louis the Pious*, **843. Quoted in R. McKitterick (ed.),** *The Times: Mapping History – Medieval World*, **Times Books, 2003, p. 41.**

[4] **Juvaini,** *History of the World-Conqueror*, **c. 1260. Adapted from R. McKitterick (ed.),** *The Times: Mapping History – Medieval World*, **Times Books, 2003, p. 175.**

[5] **Daniel of Beccles,** *The Book of the Civilised Man*, **thirteenth century. Quoted in D. Danziger and J. Gillingham,** *1215 – The Year of Magna Carta*, **Hodder and Stoughton, 2003, p. 17.**

[6] **Ambroise, a Norman eyewitness jongleur (minstrel). Modern translation in J. Riley-Smith (ed.),** *Atlas of the Crusades*, **Times Books, 1990, p. 65.**

[7] **Jean Froissart, a fourteenth century Flemish writer, in** *Froissart's Chronicles.*

[8] **Original in Middle English appeared in P. C. Jupp and C. Gittings,** *Death in England*, **Manchester University Press, 1999, p. 121.**

Glossary

amulet   A small magic object

Angles   People from Germany and Denmark who settled in Britain from around A.D. 400

barbarian   An ancient Greek word used by Romans and later Europeans to describe foreigners. It suggests that foreigners are wild, brutal, and savage.

Basque   A member of a group living in the western Pyrenees Mountains between today's Spain and France

caravans   Travelers who group together to help each other, usually in a hostile region, such as a desert

concentric   Having more than one set of walls surrounding a central donjon

crossbow   A powerful bow-shaped weapon that fired short, thick arrows, called quarels, or bolts

Crusades   Wars fought between Christians and Muslims, pagans, or heretics

donjons   Strong central towers of a castle, also called keeps

estates   Large areas of land owned by one family

falconry   Hunting using hawks to attack prey

Franks/Frankish   People who lived in France and the Netherlands from around A.D. 500 onward

garderobes   Lavatories (literally "wardrobes," closets), usually with a stone bench with a hole over a drain that led via the castle wall to the moat

garrison   Soldiers living in a castle, to guard it

Germanic   Related to German-speaking peoples, such as the Goths, Visigoths, and Franks, who moved into western Europe in the later centuries of the Roman Empire and set up several new kingdoms after the fall of the western Roman Empire

Goths   A Germanic people who invaded the Roman Empire early in the Christian era

herald   A person who proclaims news or delivers messages to individuals

heretics   Christians with beliefs not approved by Church leaders

Holy Roman Empire   A confederation of mostly German and Italian regions that lasted from the ninth century until 1806

Huns   A nomadic people from Central Asia who, under Attila, invaded central and eastern Europe in about A.D. 450

jongleur   A medieval entertainer who usually could juggle, do acrobatics, recite poems, or play a musical instrument

knights   Well-trained warriors, mostly from high-ranking families

Kurd/Kurdish   A member of a group of people that inhabits a region that now includes parts of Turkey, Iraq, Iran, Syria, Armenia, and Azerbaijan. Most Kurds are Muslims.

longbows   Vertical hand-drawn bows usually made of yew wood

Magyars   A nomadic people from Russia who migrated to Hungary about A.D. 1000

medieval   A word that relates to and describes the Middle Ages

mercenary   A professional soldier who fights for anyone who pays him

migrate   To move from one place to another

moats   Deep ditches filled with water

Mongols   Nomadic tribes from Central Asia

Muslims   Followers of Islam who believe that Muhammad was a prophet of God (Allah)

nomadic   Relating to people who move from place to place

pagans   A word used by Christians and Muslims to describe people who do not share their faith

parliaments   Conferences to discuss public affairs, or the organization of political groups to form a government

peasants   Country people; poor farmers

pitchfork   A farming tool that consists of a big two- or three-pronged fork at the end of a long handle

rank   A position in society

ransom   Money paid to set prisoners free

Roman Empire   The people and lands that belonged to ancient Rome, consisting of most of southern Europe and northern Africa from Britain to the Middle East

Saxons   A people from southern Germany who moved to England after about A.D. 400

Scandinavia   The nations of northern Europe that now include Denmark, Norway, Sweden, and Finland

shock troops   Troops whose mission was to deliver a sudden crushing blow to the enemy

siege   A military blockade of a city or fortress, cutting it off from outside help

squires   Young men training to be a knight; a knight's assistant.

tournaments   Mock battles fought as entertainment

Vandals   An eastern Germanic people who invaded Spain and Rome in the early Christian period

Vikings   A warlike people from Scandinavia who invaded areas of Europe and Russia in the ninth and tenth centuries

Visigoths   A division of Goths who came from regions of western Germany

Books:

Bartlett, Robert. *Medieval Panorama*. New York: Thames and Hudson, 2001.

Gravett, Christopher. *Castle* (Eyewitness Books). New York: DK Publishing, 2002.

Gravett, Christopher. *The World of the Medieval Knight.* New York: Peter Bedrick Books, 1996.

Langley, Andrew. *Medieval Life* (Eyewitness Books). New York: DK Publishing, 2004.

Loyn, H. R. (ed.). *The Middle Ages, A Concise Encyclopaedia*. New York: Thames and Hudson, 1991.

Macdonald, Fiona. *You Wouldn't Want to be a Medieval Knight*. New York: Franklin Watts, 2004.

Web Sites:

Castles on the Web

www.castlesontheweb.com

This well illustrated web site enables you to visit castles, abbeys, and churches throughout Europe, the Middle East, and Japan. You can find out about myths and legends as well.

The Middle Ages

www.learner.org/exhibits/middleages

This web site provides an extensive look at various aspects of daily life in the Middle Ages with links to information about feudal life, homes, religion, clothing, town life, arts, and entertainment.

Middle Ages Art and Armor

www.metmuseum.org

The Metropolitan Museum of Art (New York) web site has links to information about armor and medieval works of art including those at The Cloisters, which is a part of the museum devoted to medieval art.

Videos/DVDs:

Great Castles of Europe. Discovery Communication, 1998 (VHS).

Knights & Armor. A & E Entertainment, 1995 (VHS, DVD).

The Knights Templar. Bfs Entertainment/Mu, 2002 (VHS, DVD).

Medieval Siege (*Secrets of Lost Empires,* series 2). WGBH, 2004 (VHS, DVD).

The Middle Ages. Goldhil Video, 2001 (VHS).